AF605507

PENGUIN BOOKS

UK | USA | Canada | Ireland | Australia
India | New Zealand | South Africa | China

Penguin Random House Australia is part of the Penguin Random House group of companies whose addresses can be found at global.penguinrandomhouse.com.

First published by Penguin, an imprint of Penguin Random House Australia Pty Ltd, in 2025

Cover design and illustrations by Kristy Lund-White © Penguin Random House Australia Pty Ltd

Internal design by Rebecca King © Penguin Random House Australia Pty Ltd

Printed in China

A catalogue record for this
book is available from the
National Library of Australia

ISBN 978 1 76135 872 2 (Paperback)

penguin.com.au

We at Penguin Random House Australia acknowledge that Aboriginal and Torres Strait Islander peoples are the Traditional Custodians and the first storytellers of the lands on which we live and work. We honour Aboriginal and Torres Strait Islander peoples' continuous connection to Country, waters, skies and communities. We celebrate Aboriginal and Torres Strait Islander stories, traditions and living cultures; and we pay our respects to Elders past and present.

Bookish.

PENGUIN BOOKS

This book belongs to

To Be Read

To Be Read

	Title
1	
2	
3	
4	
5	
6	
7	
8	
9	
10	
11	
12	
13	
14	
15	
16	
17	
18	
19	
20	
21	
22	
23	
24	
25	

To Be Read

To Be Read

	Title
26	
27	
28	
29	
30	
31	
32	
33	
34	
35	
36	
37	
38	
39	
40	
41	
42	
43	
44	
45	
46	
47	
48	
49	
50	

Upcoming Releases

January

February

March

Upcoming Releases

April

May

June

Upcoming Releases

July

August

September

Upcoming Releases

October

November

December

Daily Reading Tracker

	J	F	M	A	M	J
1						
2						
3						
4						
5						
6						
7						
8						
9						
10						
11						
12						
13						
14						
15						
16						
17						
18						
19						
20						
21						
22						
23						
24						
25						
26						
27						
28						
29						
30						
31						

Daily Reading Tracker

	J	A	S	O	N	D
1						
2						
3						
4						
5						
6						
7						
8						
9						
10						
11						
12						
13						
14						
15						
16						
17						
18						
19						
20						
21						
22						
23						
24						
25						
26						
27						
28						
29						
30						
31						

‘A room
without books
is like a body
without a soul.’

– *Cicero*

Book Review

Title:

Author:

Genre:

Tropes:

Rating: ☆ ☆ ☆ ☆ ☆

✦ Book Review ✦

Title:

Author:

Genre:

Tropes:

Rating: ☆ ☆ ☆ ☆ ☆

Book Review

Title:

Author:

Genre:

Tropes:

Rating: ☆ ☆ ☆ ☆ ☆

Book Review

Title:

Author:

Genre:

Tropes:

Rating: ☆ ☆ ☆ ☆ ☆

Book Review

Title:

Author:

Genre:

Tropes:

Rating: ☆☆☆☆☆

✦✦ Book Review ✦✦

Title:

Author:

Genre:

Tropes:

Rating: ☆☆☆☆☆

Book Review

Title:

Author:

Genre:

Tropes:

Rating: ☆ ☆ ☆ ☆ ☆

Book Review

Title:

Author:

Genre:

Tropes:

Rating: ☆ ☆ ☆ ☆ ☆

✦ Book Review ✦

Title:

Author:

Genre:

Tropes:

Rating: ☆ ☆ ☆ ☆ ☆

Book Review

Title:

Author:

Genre:

Tropes:

Rating: ☆ ☆ ☆ ☆ ☆

Book Review

Title:

Author:

Genre:

Tropes:

Rating: ☆ ☆ ☆ ☆ ☆

Book Review

Title:

Author:

Genre:

Tropes:

Rating: ☆ ☆ ☆ ☆ ☆

Book Review

Title:

Author:

Genre:

Tropes:

Rating: ☆☆☆☆☆

Book Review

Title:

Author:

Genre:

Tropes:

Rating: ☆ ☆ ☆ ☆ ☆

Book Review

Title:

Author:

Genre:

Tropes:

Rating: ☆ ☆ ☆ ☆ ☆

Book Review

Title:

Author:

Genre:

Tropes:

Rating: ☆ ☆ ☆ ☆ ☆

Book Review

Title:

Author:

Genre:

Tropes:

Rating: ☆ ☆ ☆ ☆ ☆

✦ Book Review ✦

Title:

Author:

Genre:

Tropes:

Rating: ☆ ☆ ☆ ☆ ☆

Book Review

Title:

Author:

Genre:

Tropes:

Rating: ☆☆☆☆☆

✦ Book Review ✦

Title:

Author:

Genre:

Tropes:

Rating: ☆ ☆ ☆ ☆ ☆

✦ Book Review ✦

Title:

Author:

Genre:

Tropes:

Rating: ☆ ☆ ☆ ☆ ☆

Book Review

Title:

Author:

Genre:

Tropes:

Rating: ☆☆☆☆☆

Book Review

Title:

Author:

Genre:

Tropes:

Rating: ☆ ☆ ☆ ☆ ☆

Book Review

Title:

Author:

Genre:

Tropes:

Rating: ☆ ☆ ☆ ☆ ☆

Book Review

Title:

Author:

Genre:

Tropes:

Rating: ☆ ☆ ☆ ☆ ☆

✦✦ Book Review ✦✦

Title:

Author:

Genre:

Tropes:

Rating: ☆ ☆ ☆ ☆ ☆

Book Review

Title:

Author:

Genre:

Tropes:

Rating: ☆ ☆ ☆ ☆ ☆

Book Review

Title:

Author:

Genre:

Tropes:

Rating: ☆☆☆☆☆

✦ Book Review ✦

Title:

Author:

Genre:

Tropes:

Rating: ☆ ☆ ☆ ☆ ☆

✦✦ Book Review ✦✦

Title:

Author:

Genre:

Tropes:

Rating: ☆☆☆☆☆

✦ Book Review ✦

Title:

Author:

Genre:

Tropes:

Rating: ☆ ☆ ☆ ☆ ☆

Book Review

Title:

Author:

Genre:

Tropes:

Rating: ☆ ☆ ☆ ☆ ☆

Book Review

Title:

Author:

Genre:

Tropes:

Rating: ☆ ☆ ☆ ☆ ☆

Book Review

Title:

Author:

Genre:

Tropes:

Rating: ☆☆☆☆☆

Book Review

Title:

Author:

Genre:

Tropes:

Rating: ☆ ☆ ☆ ☆ ☆

Book Review

Title:

Author:

Genre:

Tropes:

Rating: ☆☆☆☆☆

Book Review

Title:

Author:

Genre:

Tropes:

Rating: ☆☆☆☆☆

Book Review

Title:

Author:

Genre:

Tropes:

Rating: ☆ ☆ ☆ ☆ ☆

✦ Book Review ✦

Title:

Author:

Genre:

Tropes:

Rating: ☆ ☆ ☆ ☆ ☆

✦✦ Book Review ✦✦

Title:

Author:

Genre:

Tropes:

Rating: ☆ ☆ ☆ ☆ ☆

Book Review

Title:

Author:

Genre:

Tropes:

Rating: ☆ ☆ ☆ ☆ ☆

Book Review

Title:

Author:

Genre:

Tropes:

Rating: ☆ ☆ ☆ ☆ ☆

Book Review

Title:

Author:

Genre:

Tropes:

Rating: ☆ ☆ ☆ ☆ ☆

Book Review

Title:

Author:

Genre:

Tropes:

Rating: ☆ ☆ ☆ ☆ ☆

✦ Book Review ✦

Title:

Author:

Genre:

Tropes:

Rating: ☆☆☆☆☆

✦ Book Review ✦

Title:

Author:

Genre:

Tropes:

Rating: ☆ ☆ ☆ ☆ ☆

✦ Book Review ✦

Title:

Author:

Genre:

Tropes:

Rating: ☆ ☆ ☆ ☆ ☆

✦ Book Review ✦

Title:

Author:

Genre:

Tropes:

Rating: ☆ ☆ ☆ ☆ ☆

Book Review

Title:

Author:

Genre:

Tropes:

Rating: ☆ ☆ ☆ ☆ ☆

✦ Book Review ✦

Title:

Author:

Genre:

Tropes:

Rating: ☆ ☆ ☆ ☆ ☆

Book Review

Title:

Author:

Genre:

Tropes:

Rating: ☆☆☆☆☆

✦ Book Review ✦

Title:

Author:

Genre:

Tropes:

Rating: ☆ ☆ ☆ ☆ ☆

Book Review

Title:

Author:

Genre:

Tropes:

Rating: ☆ ☆ ☆ ☆ ☆

Book Review

Title:

Author:

Genre:

Tropes:

Rating: ☆ ☆ ☆ ☆ ☆

Book Review

Title:

Author:

Genre:

Tropes:

Rating: ☆ ☆ ☆ ☆ ☆

Book Review

Title:

Author:

Genre:

Tropes:

Rating: ☆ ☆ ☆ ☆ ☆

Book Review

Title:

Author:

Genre:

Tropes:

Rating: ☆ ☆ ☆ ☆ ☆

✦ Book Review ✦

Title:

Author:

Genre:

Tropes:

Rating: ☆ ☆ ☆ ☆ ☆

✦✦ Book Review ✦✦

Title:

Author:

Genre:

Tropes:

Rating: ☆☆☆☆☆

Book Review

Title:

Author:

Genre:

Tropes:

Rating: ☆ ☆ ☆ ☆ ☆

Book Review

Title:

Author:

Genre:

Tropes:

Rating: ☆ ☆ ☆ ☆ ☆

✦ Book Review ✦

Title:

Author:

Genre:

Tropes:

Rating: ☆ ☆ ☆ ☆ ☆

Book Review

Title:

Author:

Genre:

Tropes:

Rating: ☆ ☆ ☆ ☆ ☆

Book Review

Title:

Author:

Genre:

Tropes:

Rating: ☆ ☆ ☆ ☆ ☆

Book Review

Title:

Author:

Genre:

Tropes:

Rating: ☆ ☆ ☆ ☆ ☆

Book Review

Title:

Author:

Genre:

Tropes:

Rating: ☆ ☆ ☆ ☆ ☆

Book Review

Title:

Author:

Genre:

Tropes:

Rating: ☆ ☆ ☆ ☆ ☆

✦✦ Book Review ✦✦

Title:

Author:

Genre:

Tropes:

Rating: ☆ ☆ ☆ ☆ ☆

‘There is no friend as loyal as a book.’

– Ernest Hemingway

Book Review

Title:

Author:

Genre:

Tropes:

Rating: ☆ ☆ ☆ ☆ ☆

Book Review

Title:

Author:

Genre:

Tropes:

Rating: ☆ ☆ ☆ ☆ ☆

Book Review

Title:

Author:

Genre:

Tropes:

Rating: ☆ ☆ ☆ ☆ ☆

Book Review

Title:

Author:

Genre:

Tropes:

Rating: ☆☆☆☆☆

✦✦ Book Review ✦✦

Title:

Author:

Genre:

Tropes:

Rating: ☆ ☆ ☆ ☆ ☆

Book Review

Title:

Author:

Genre:

Tropes:

Rating: ☆☆☆☆☆

Book Review

Title:

Author:

Genre:

Tropes:

Rating: ☆ ☆ ☆ ☆ ☆

Book Review

Title:

Author:

Genre:

Tropes:

Rating: ☆ ☆ ☆ ☆ ☆

Book Review

Title:

Author:

Genre:

Tropes:

Rating: ☆ ☆ ☆ ☆ ☆

Book Review

Title:

Author:

Genre:

Tropes:

Rating: ☆ ☆ ☆ ☆ ☆

Book Review

Title:

Author:

Genre:

Tropes:

Rating: ☆ ☆ ☆ ☆ ☆

Book Review

Title:

Author:

Genre:

Tropes:

Rating: ☆ ☆ ☆ ☆ ☆

Book Review

Title:

Author:

Genre:

Tropes:

Rating: ☆ ☆ ☆ ☆ ☆

✦ Book Review ✦

Title:

Author:

Genre:

Tropes:

Rating: ☆ ☆ ☆ ☆ ☆

✦ Book Review ✦

Title:

Author:

Genre:

Tropes:

Rating: ☆ ☆ ☆ ☆ ☆

Book Review

Title:

Author:

Genre:

Tropes:

Rating: ☆ ☆ ☆ ☆ ☆

Book Review

Title:

Author:

Genre:

Tropes:

Rating: ☆ ☆ ☆ ☆ ☆

Book Review

Title:

Author:

Genre:

Tropes:

Rating: ☆ ☆ ☆ ☆ ☆

Book Review

Title:

Author:

Genre:

Tropes:

Rating: ☆ ☆ ☆ ☆ ☆

Book Review

Title:

Author:

Genre:

Tropes:

Rating: ☆ ☆ ☆ ☆ ☆

Book Review

Title:

Author:

Genre:

Tropes:

Rating: ☆ ☆ ☆ ☆ ☆

Book Review

Title:

Author:

Genre:

Tropes:

Rating: ☆ ☆ ☆ ☆ ☆

Book Review

Title:

Author:

Genre:

Tropes:

Rating: ☆ ☆ ☆ ☆ ☆

Book Review

Title:

Author:

Genre:

Tropes:

Rating: ☆☆☆☆☆

Book Review

Title:

Author:

Genre:

Tropes:

Rating: ☆ ☆ ☆ ☆ ☆

Book Review

Title:

Author:

Genre:

Tropes:

Rating: ☆ ☆ ☆ ☆ ☆

Book Review

Title:

Author:

Genre:

Tropes:

Rating: ☆☆☆☆☆

Book Review

Title:

Author:

Genre:

Tropes:

Rating: ☆ ☆ ☆ ☆ ☆

Book Review

Title:

Author:

Genre:

Tropes:

Rating: ☆☆☆☆☆

Book Review

Title:

Author:

Genre:

Tropes:

Rating: ☆ ☆ ☆ ☆ ☆

Book Review

Title:

Author:

Genre:

Tropes:

Rating: ☆ ☆ ☆ ☆ ☆

✦✦ Book Review ✦✦

Title:

Author:

Genre:

Tropes:

Rating: ☆ ☆ ☆ ☆ ☆

Book Review

Title:

Author:

Genre:

Tropes:

Rating: ☆☆☆☆☆

✦ Book Review ✦

Title:

Author:

Genre:

Tropes:

Rating: ☆ ☆ ☆ ☆ ☆

Book Review

Title:

Author:

Genre:

Tropes:

Rating: ☆ ☆ ☆ ☆ ☆

Book Review

Title:

Author:

Genre:

Tropes:

Rating: ☆☆☆☆☆

Book Review

Title:

Author:

Genre:

Tropes:

Rating: ☆ ☆ ☆ ☆ ☆

Book Review

Title:

Author:

Genre:

Tropes:

Rating: ☆ ☆ ☆ ☆ ☆

Book Review

Title:

Author:

Genre:

Tropes:

Rating: ☆ ☆ ☆ ☆ ☆

Book Review

Title:

Author:

Genre:

Tropes:

Rating: ☆ ☆ ☆ ☆ ☆

✦ Book Review ✦

Title:

Author:

Genre:

Tropes:

Rating: ☆ ☆ ☆ ☆ ☆

Book Review

Title:

Author:

Genre:

Tropes:

Rating: ☆ ☆ ☆ ☆ ☆

Book Review

Title:

Author:

Genre:

Tropes:

Rating: ☆ ☆ ☆ ☆ ☆

Book Review

Title:

Author:

Genre:

Tropes:

Rating: ☆ ☆ ☆ ☆ ☆

Book Review

Title:

Author:

Genre:

Tropes:

Rating: ☆☆☆☆☆

✦ Book Review ✦

Title:

Author:

Genre:

Tropes:

Rating: ☆ ☆ ☆ ☆ ☆

Book Review

Title:

Author:

Genre:

Tropes:

Rating: ☆ ☆ ☆ ☆ ☆

✦ Book Review ✦

Title:

Author:

Genre:

Tropes:

Rating: ☆ ☆ ☆ ☆ ☆

Book Review

Title:

Author:

Genre:

Tropes:

Rating: ☆ ☆ ☆ ☆ ☆

Book Review

Title:

Author:

Genre:

Tropes:

Rating: ☆ ☆ ☆ ☆ ☆

Book Review

Title:

Author:

Genre:

Tropes:

Rating: ☆☆☆☆☆

Book Review

Title:

Author:

Genre:

Tropes:

Rating: ☆ ☆ ☆ ☆ ☆

Book Review

Title:

Author:

Genre:

Tropes:

Rating: ☆ ☆ ☆ ☆ ☆

Book Review

Title:

Author:

Genre:

Tropes:

Rating: ☆ ☆ ☆ ☆ ☆

Book Review

Title:

Author:

Genre:

Tropes:

Rating: ☆ ☆ ☆ ☆ ☆

Book Review

Title:

Author:

Genre:

Tropes:

Rating: ☆☆☆☆☆

Book Review

Title:

Author:

Genre:

Tropes:

Rating: ☆ ☆ ☆ ☆ ☆

✦ Book Review ✦

Title:

Author:

Genre:

Tropes:

Rating: ☆☆☆☆☆

✦ Book Review ✦

Title:

Author:

Genre:

Tropes:

Rating: ☆ ☆ ☆ ☆ ☆

Book Review

Title:

Author:

Genre:

Tropes:

Rating: ☆ ☆ ☆ ☆ ☆

Book Review

Title:

Author:

Genre:

Tropes:

Rating: ☆ ☆ ☆ ☆ ☆

✦✦ Book Review ✦✦

Title:

Author:

Genre:

Tropes:

Rating: ☆☆☆☆☆

✦✦ Book Review ✦✦

Title:

Author:

Genre:

Tropes:

Rating: ☆☆☆☆☆

✦✦ Book Review ✦✦

Title:

Author:

Genre:

Tropes:

Rating: ☆ ☆ ☆ ☆ ☆

Book Review

Title:

Author:

Genre:

Tropes:

Rating: ☆☆☆☆☆

✦ Book Review ✦

Title:

Author:

Genre:

Tropes:

Rating: ☆ ☆ ☆ ☆ ☆

Book Review

Title:

Author:

Genre:

Tropes:

Rating: ☆ ☆ ☆ ☆ ☆

Book Review

Title:

Author:

Genre:

Tropes:

Rating: ☆ ☆ ☆ ☆ ☆

‘Books are a uniquely portable magic.’

– Stephen King

Book Bingo

Manga	Award-winning	A new release
A book that became a movie	A book that scares you	Fantasy genre
A book with a one-word title	Crime genre	A 600+ page book
Re-read an old favourite	A neurodiverse main character	LGBTQI+ author
A debut novel	A book of short stories	BIPOC author

Make Your Own Book Bingo

‘Books are
the mirrors
of the soul.’

– *Virginia Woolf*

25 Must Read Classics Checklist

Jane Eyre **Charlotte Brontë**	Pride and Prejudice **Jane Austen**	Wuthering Heights **Emily Brontë**	The Three Musketeers **Alexandre Dumas**	Don Quixote **Miguel De Cervantes**
Anna Karenina **Leo Tolstoy**	The Adventures of Huckleberry Finn **Mark Twain**	Romeo and Juliet **William Shakespeare**	Middlemarch **George Eliot**	Treasure Island **Robert Louis Stevenson**
Little Women **Louisa May Alcott**	The Picture of Dorian Gray **Oscar Wilde**	The Strange Case of Dr Jekyll and Mr Hyde **Robert Louis Stevenson**	Alice's Adventures in Wonderland **Lewis Carroll**	Peter Pan **JM Barrie**
Gulliver's Travels **Jonathan Swift**	Tess of the D'Urbervilles **Thomas Hardy**	Great Expectations **Charles Dickens**	The Count of Monte Cristo **Alexandre Dumas**	Dracula **Bram Stoker**
Twenty Thousand Leagues Under the Sea **Jules Verne**	Moby-Dick **Herman Melville**	Macbeth **William Shakespeare**	Far From the Madding Crowd **Thomas Hardy**	Frankenstein **Mary Shelley**

Choose Your Own Must Read Classics

25 Must Read Modern Classics Checklist

To Kill a Mockingbird **Harper Lee**	Lord of the Flies **William Golding**	The Great Gatsby **F Scott Fitzgerald**	The Outsiders **SE Hinton**	The Book Thief **Markus Zusak**
The Diary of a Young Girl **Anne Frank**	The Hobbit **JRR Tolkien**	The Lion, the Witch and the Wardrobe **CS Lewis**	Animal Farm **George Orwell**	Brave New World **Aldous Huxley**
The Old Man and the Sea **Ernest Hemingway**	Fahrenheit 451 **Ray Bradbury**	Of Mice and Men **John Steinbeck**	Rebecca **Daphne du Maurier**	Beloved **Toni Morrison**
Slaughterhouse-Five **Kurt Vonnegut**	Atonement **Ian McEwan**	1984 **George Orwell**	Catch-22 **Joseph Heller**	Life of Pi **Yann Martel**
The Metamorphosis **Franz Kafka**	Heart of Darkness **Joseph Conrad**	The Secret History **Donna Tartt**	The Handmaid's Tale **Margaret Atwood**	Mrs Dalloway **Virginia Woolf**

Choose Your Own Must Read Modern Classics

Did Not Finish

Did Not Finish

Did Not Finish

Did Not Finish

Favourite Books

Favourite Books

Favourite Books

✦ Favourite Books ✦

☆☆☆☆☆ ☆☆☆☆☆ ☆☆☆☆☆

☆☆☆☆☆ ☆☆☆☆☆ ☆☆☆☆☆

☆☆☆☆☆ ☆☆☆☆☆ ☆☆☆☆☆

Favourite Books

Favourite Books

‘We lose ourselves in books, we find ourselves there too.’

– *Anonymous*